NORMANDY TRAVEL GUIDE 2024

Explore Must-see Attractions, Where to Stay,
Budget-Friendly Tips, Things to do, Places to
Visit and What to Eat in France's Gem

Emmaline Gill

Table of Contents

Chapter 1: Planning Your Trip to Normandy

My Normandy Travel Experience

In 2024, I fulfilled my long-standing desire to explore Normandy, the region in northern France renowned for its historical significance, cultural richness, and natural allure. This area witnessed the pivotal D-Day landings in 1944, inspired renowned impressionist painters, and is celebrated for producing delectable cheeses, ciders, and crepes. The opportunity to visit Normandy was met with overwhelming joy, setting the stage for an eagerly anticipated exploration.

Commencing my journey in Rouen, the capital of Normandy, I was captivated by the Gothic cathedral, the medieval old town, and a museum dedicated to Joan of Arc. The next stop was Honfleur, a quaint port town charmed by its colorful houses, lively harbor, and vibrant art galleries. Subsequently, I ventured to the elegant seaside resorts of Deauville and Trouville, where the combination of beach relaxation, chic boutique shopping, and fresh seafood created a delightful experience.

The Normandy coast beckoned next, offering a profound encounter with the history and beauty of the

D-Day beaches. Visits to the American Cemetery, Pointe du Hoc, Omaha Beach, and Arromanches provided insights into the courage and sacrifice of the Allied soldiers. The trip went on to Bayeux, where the well-known tapestry showing the Norman conquest of England in 1066 displayed extraordinary, nearly a millennium-old artistry.

A visit to the iconic Mont Saint-Michel followed, a medieval fortress rising majestically from the sea. The sight of the abbey, the cloister, and the gardens, coupled with views of the bay, tides, and surrounding countryside, created a magical experience. Spending a night on the island felt like a journey back in time.

The final leg of my trip unfolded in Caen, the largest city in Normandy, where exploration led me to castles, churches, and museums. The Memorial for Peace, a poignant and informative museum covering 20th-century history, left a lasting impression. Culminating the journey was an indulgence in the diverse and delicious local cuisine, including camembert, livarot, pont-l'évêque, Calvados, cider, and crepes – all proudly crafted in Normandy.

The profound and enchanting experience in Normandy inspired the creation of this travel guide, a heartfelt recommendation for those seeking an unforgettable vacation. Normandy's allure is multifaceted, promising a rich tapestry of history, culture, and culinary delights. The anticipation of a return visit is a testament to the region's enduring charm.

1.1 Best Time to Visit

Normandy, nestled in the northern expanse of France, unfolds as a captivating region that promises travelers a diverse and enriching experience. Whether one's interests lean toward history, culture, nature, or gastronomy, Normandy welcomes all. Yet, the question persists – When would be the best time to travel to this fascinating location?

Factors such as weather, events, and attractions play pivotal roles in determining the ideal time for a visit. Normandy boasts a temperate climate with four distinct seasons, ranging from an average of 5°C in winter to 20°C in summer. The weather, albeit changeable, adds an element of unpredictability, urging travelers to pack layers and a raincoat. Spring (April-May) and autumn (September-October) emerge as prime seasons, offering mild weather, blooming flowers, and a picturesque landscape.

Summer (June-August) signifies the peak season, featuring warmer days and drawing larger crowds and higher prices. Winter (November-March) marks the low season, characterized by colder, wetter days, yet offering respite through fewer tourists and lower rates. Normandy's calendar is peppered with events and festivals celebrating its rich history, culture, and traditions. Some notable events include:

1. The D-Day Festival: This event, which takes place from June 1 to June 16, celebrates the Battle of Normandy's 80th anniversary in 2024 as well as the D-Day landings. Ceremonies, concerts, exhibitions, reenactments, and fireworks culminate in the international ceremony on Omaha Beach on June 6.

2. The Impressionist Festival: A biennial celebration from April to September, this festival pays homage to the impressionist movement and its connection to Normandy. The 2024 edition, themed "Impressionism and the Sea," features exhibitions, concerts, workshops, conferences, and guided tours.

3. The Cheese Festival: An annual affair in May, this festival showcases Normandy's delectable cheeses, including camembert, livarot, and pont-l'évêque. Tastings, markets, demonstrations, and competitions occur in various locations each year.

Normandy's allure extends beyond events to its array of attractions, including:

1. The D-Day Beaches: These historic beaches witnessed the Allied forces landing on June 6, 1944, marking a pivotal historical moment. Museums, cemeteries, and memorials tell the story of this liberation.

2. Mont Saint-Michel: A UNESCO World Heritage Site, this medieval island abbey rises dramatically from the sea. Exploring the causeway, climbing steep steps, and wandering through the abbey, cloister, and gardens offer a magical experience.

3. Monet's Garden: This garden, where Claude Monet lived and worked, showcases colorful flowers, water lilies, and the iconic Japanese bridge. Monet's house, studio, and original artworks add to the artistic allure.

In essence, Normandy stands as an extraordinary destination, welcoming visitors throughout the year. However, spring is the recommended time to explore this picturesque region for an optimal experience marked by pleasant weather, smaller crowds, and abundant events. As the flowers bloom, trees blossom, and birds serenade, Normandy awaits your visit. Set out on your adventure right now and be ready to be enthralled with the splendors of this extraordinary area!

1.2 Budgeting Your Trip

Normandy, a treasure trove of history, culture, and natural splendor, can handle your budget. By strategically planning and making savvy choices, you can relish a remarkable trip to Normandy in 2024 without breaking the bank. Here are some practical tips to budget your Normandy expedition:

Transportation: Opting for the train from Paris emerges as the most economical means, with tickets as low as €15 one-way when booked in advance during off-peak hours. The two-hour journey leads you to Caen, Rouen, or Le Havre, where local trains or buses can efficiently navigate the region. Alternatively, renting a car offers flexibility, though it involves additional costs like tolls, gas (approximately €10 per day), and parking (around €5). Guided tours, while convenient, might limit spontaneity and freedom, costing around €200 per person for a two-day trip or €400 for a four-day journey.

Accommodation: Normandy provides various accommodation options, from quaint bed and breakfasts to luxurious hotels. A double room's average price is €80 per night, but online bookings or staying in less popular areas can yield more budget-friendly options. Charming B&Bs in Bayeux or modern hotels in

Caen can be secured for €60 or €50 per night, respectively. Hostels, campsites, or Airbnb rentals offer even more economical choices, starting at €20 per night.

Food: Normandy's renowned cuisine can be savored affordably, featuring seafood, cheese, cider, and apple products. Local markets showcase fresh and budget-friendly produce, with meals costing around €10 per person, including sandwiches and salads. Dinner options include fixed-price menus or "menu du jour" at local restaurants, offering regional specialties like moules-frites and camembert cheese for approximately €15 per person, excluding drinks. For a splurge, Michelin-starred restaurants like La Marine or L'Auberge du Vieux Puits offer exquisite dishes at a higher cost, around €100 per person or more.

Attractions: Normandy boasts a plethora of attractions catering to diverse interests. Popular sites include the D-Day beaches and museums, Mont Saint-Michel, Monet's Garden in Giverny, the Bayeux Tapestry, and the Normandy Bridge. Entrance fees range from €5.40 to €10 per person, with some attractions, like the American Cemetery in Colleville-sur-Mer, being free of charge. Hidden gems and off-the-beaten-path places await exploration, inviting you to discover Normandy at your own pace and budget.

Normandy extends an invitation for exploration, learning, and enjoyment, accommodating various preferences and budgets. Whether seeking a relaxing retreat, cultural immersion, or adventurous escapade, Normandy's charm promises an enriching experience without financial strain.

1.3 Travel Insurance

Normandy, an enchanting and historically rich region in France, beckons travelers with its breathtaking landscapes, picturesque villages, and monumental landmarks. It's a haven for adventure enthusiasts, offering many activities such as hiking, cycling, kayaking, sailing, and more. While the allure of Normandy is undeniable, unforeseen circumstances can disrupt your vacation, emphasizing the need for a reliable travel insurance policy tailored to your specific requirements.

Travel insurance is strongly advised for a vacation to Normandy, even if it is not required. It covers a variety of circumstances, such as:

1. Trip Cancellation or Interruption: Reimbursement for non-refundable costs due to unforeseen circumstances like illness, injury, family member's death, natural disasters, or travel bans.

2. Medical Expenses: Coverage for medical treatment, hospitalization, medication, and transportation in case of sickness or injury during the trip, particularly crucial for adventurous activities not covered by regular health insurance or the European Health Insurance Card (EHIC).

3. Emergency Evacuation and Repatriation: Financial coverage for transportation costs and related services if evacuation to a safer location or repatriation to your home country becomes necessary due to a severe medical condition or security threat.

4. Baggage and Personal Effects: Compensation for lost, stolen, or damaged luggage or personal belongings, covering their value or the cost of repair or replacement.

5. Personal Liability: Coverage for legal expenses and compensation claims arising from injury or damage caused to others or their property during the trip.

With numerous travel insurance providers and plans available, careful consideration is essential. Factors to assess include:

- **Coverage Limits and Exclusions**: Ensure the policy aligns with your needs and verifies what is not covered or requires additional fees or approval.
- **Excess or Deductible:** The amount payable out of pocket before insurance activation; balancing a higher excess reduces the premium but lessens coverage.

- **Claim Process and Customer Service**: Evaluate the ease and speed of filing claims, responsiveness, and helpfulness of customer service.
- **Reviews and Ratings:** Peruse customer feedback and testimonials, gauging the quality and reliability of the service.

A standout travel insurance provider is World Nomads, which is recognized for its flexibility and comprehensive plans catering to diverse travelers. Covering over 200+ activities, including adventure sports often excluded by other policies, World Nomads allows online policy management, 24/7 emergency assistance, and online claims from any global location. The company also supports local communities by facilitating donations during policy purchases.

To obtain a quote from World Nomads, furnish details such as your country of residence, destination(s), trip dates, and age. Choose between the Standard and Explorer plans, each offering varying coverage and premiums. Optional extras, such as high-value items, winter sports, or rental car excess, can be added. Their [website] has A detailed plan comparison (https://www.worldnomads.com/travel-insurance).

Travel insurance is not a luxury but a necessity. It may save you a great deal of money, time, and trouble in the event that something goes wrong when traveling. It can also give you peace of mind and confidence to enjoy your trip. So remember to buy a suitable travel insurance policy before you head to Normandy, and have a wonderful and safe journey!

1.4 Visa Requirements

Before embarking on your journey to Normandy, ensuring you possess the appropriate visa to enter France is crucial. Depending on your country, the reason for your travel, and the length of your stay, you may or may not need a visa. Here are comprehensive guidelines to assist you in planning your trip:

European Union (EU) Citizens: A valid passport or national identity card suffices if you are a citizen of the European Union, the European Economic Area (EEA), Switzerland, or the United Kingdom. There's no need for a visa, and you can stay in France without restrictions.

Visa-Exempt Countries for Short Stays in Schengen Area: For brief visits inside the Schengen Area, citizens of 62 nations—including Australia, Canada, Japan, New Zealand, Singapore, South Korea, and the United States—are not required to have a visa. A valid passport is essential; you can stay for up to 90 days within 180 days without restrictions. Here is a link to the complete list of nations that do not require a visa.

Non-Exempt Countries: Citizens of countries not exempt from visa requirements must apply for a visa in advance at the nearest French embassy or consulate in their country of residence. In order to apply, you must fill out a form, submit the required paperwork, pay the visa application cost, and show up for an interview. The type of visa depends on the purpose and duration of the trip, including:

- **Short-Stay Visa (Schengen Visa):** Valid for up to 90 days within 180 days for tourism, business, family visits, cultural exchanges, or transit. The cost is €40 for kids ages six to twelve and €80 for adults.

- **Long-Stay Visa:** Allows stays exceeding 90 days for purposes such as study, work, family reunion, or retirement. Fees range from €99 to €269.

- **Health Care Visa:** Permits entry for medical treatment or consultation, valid for up to 90 days within 180 days. Adults pay €80, while children between the ages of six and twelve pay €40.

Additional Documents Upon Arrival: Regardless of visa status, travelers may need to present supplementary documents upon arrival, such as proof of insurance, evidence of an onward travel ticket, and accommodation details (or sufficient funds). Health screenings or security checks at the border may also be required. Preparing all necessary documents in advance is advisable to prevent entry denial or delays.

Important Note: Visa requirements for France are subject to change based on the prevailing situation and bilateral agreements between countries. Before departing, make sure you often check the [French Ministry of Foreign Affairs](link) official website for the most recent information.

Chapter 2: Must-See Attractions and Landmarks

2.1 D-Day Beaches

In order to begin the liberation of Europe from Nazi control, the Allied troops landed on the D-Day Beaches on June 6, 1944, making it one of the most significant and unforgettable places to visit in Normandy. The D-Day Beaches stretch for about 50 miles along the coast of Normandy, from Pegasus Bridge to Sainte-Mère-Eglise. Each beach has its history, landmarks, and museums that tell the story of this pivotal moment in World War II.

The D-Day Beaches are divided into five sectors, each with a codename given by the Allies: Utah, Omaha, Gold, Juno, and Sword. Each sector was assigned to a different nationality: the Americans at Utah and Omaha, the British at Gold and Sword, and the Canadians at Juno. You can visit each sector and learn about the challenges, the achievements, and the sacrifices of the soldiers who fought there.

Here are some of the highlights of each sector:

Kindly scan or click on the QR code for accurate map direction

Utah Beach: Exploring Utah Beach offers a poignant journey into history, serving as the westernmost and comparatively less defended of the five beaches. The American 4th Infantry Division, encountering minimal casualties, landed slightly off target due to robust currents. Swiftly regrouping, they seized the nearby town of Sainte-Marie-du-Mont, where a statue commemorates Brigadier General Theodore Roosevelt Jr., the leader of the first wave of troops. A visit to the Utah Beach Museum, housed in a former German bunker, provides a captivating experience. Open daily, the museum showcases artifacts, vehicles, and dioramas related to the historic landing. Operating from 9:30 am to 7 pm (April to September) and 10 am to 6 pm (October to March), with an admission fee of 9.50 euros for adults, 6 euros for children, and free entry for veterans. For more details, check and confirm from the official website [https://en.normandie-tourisme.fr/highlight/80th-anniversary-of-d-day/].

Scan the QR code or click on the link for map directions to Omaha Beach

Omaha Beach: Omaha Beach stands as the most formidable and harrowing of the five beaches, bearing witness to the intense struggle faced by the American 1st and 29th Infantry Divisions. Fierce German resistance, entrenched on the cliffs overlooking the beach, presented a formidable challenge. Compounded by delays and dispersion of landing craft due to rough seas and enemy fire, many soldiers faced fatalities or injuries before reaching the shore. Remnants of German bunkers and poignant memorials line the beach, offering solemn testimony to the courage and sacrifice displayed. Omaha Beach Museum, a repository of soldiers' uniforms, weapons, and personal items, invites visitors to delve into the historical narrative. Operating daily from 9:30 am to 6:30 pm (April to September) and 10 am to 5 pm (October to March), the museum charges an admission fee of 8.50 euros for adults and 5 euros for children, with complimentary entry for veterans.

Click on the link or scan the QR code to Gold Beach

Gold Beach: Gold Beach, situated as the intermediary among the trio of British landing sites, witnessed the arrival of the British 50th Infantry Division, supported by specialized tanks, including amphibious DD tanks and mine-clearing flail tanks. Despite encountering moderate German opposition, they successfully navigated through obstacles to advance inland. The capture of the strategic port of Arromanches marked a crucial achievement, and remnants of the artificial Mulberry harbor, pivotal in supplying Allied troops, are still visible. For those seeking a deeper understanding, the Arromanches 360° Cinema offers an immersive experience with a panoramic film recounting the events of the D-Day landings and the Battle of Normandy. Open everyday starting from 9:30 am to 6 pm (April to September) and 10 am to 5 pm (October to March), the cinema charges an admission fee of 6.50 euros for adults and 5 euros for children, while veterans enjoy complimentary entry. You can find more information on this website.

For Map direction, scan the QR code or click on the link to Juno Beach

Juno Beach: Juno Beach, positioned as the easternmost of the two Canadian landing sites, saw the Canadian 3rd Infantry Division arriving with support from the British Royal Marines and Free French commandos. The beach was heavily fortified by the Germans with mines, barbed wire, and machine guns, leading to significant Canadian casualties. Despite the formidable resistance, the Canadians displayed remarkable bravery, achieving their objectives and successfully liberating the town of Courseulles-sur-Mer. For those wanting to delve into the Canadian contribution to the war, the Juno Beach Centre is a poignant testament. Operating daily from 9:30 am to 6 pm (April to September) and 10 am to 5 pm (October to March), the center serves as both a museum and a cultural hub. Admission costs 9 euros for adults and 6 euros for children, and veterans enjoy complimentary entry.

Scan the QR code with your phone camera or click on the link for map direction to Sword Beach

Sword Beach: Sword Beach, positioned as the easternmost among the five D-Day landing sites, witnessed the British 3rd Infantry Division's arrival, supported by the French 1st Special Service Brigade, which notably included the renowned French commando Kieffer. Despite facing moderate opposition from the Germans, the British encountered challenges navigating the flooded fields and canals behind the beach. Their primary objective, the capture of the city of Caen, proved elusive. A significant point of interest is the Pegasus Bridge, a strategic location captured by the daring glider operation of the British 6th Airborne Division. Visitors can explore this historic site and delve into its stories at the Pegasus Memorial Museum. Operating daily from 10 am to 6:30 pm (April to September) and 10 am to 5 pm (October to March), the museum offers insights into the events with displays of the original bridge, gliders, and various memorabilia.

Adult admission is 8 euros, while children's admission is 5 euros and veterans enjoy complimentary entry. The D-Day Beaches stand as an essential destination for those eager to delve into the history and heroism of the Allied soldiers who bravely fought for freedom and democracy. Whether by car, bus, bike, or guided tour, visitors can explore these hallowed grounds, gaining profound insights into the pivotal events of World War II.

If you want to have an entirely immersed experience, think about taking part in the D-Day Festival Normandy, a broad range of activities honoring the anniversary of the Battle of Normandy and the D-Day landings. From June 1 to June 16, the festival features ceremonies, concerts, exhibitions, and reenactments and culminates in a grand international ceremony on Omaha Beach on June 6. This ceremony, attended by heads of state, veterans, and officials, pays solemn tribute to the courageous heroes of the liberation.

The D-Day Beaches serve as a site of historical remembrance and gratitude and embody natural beauty and cultural significance. The juxtaposition of the serene and picturesque landscape with the poignant events that transpired creates a powerful experience. Visitors will undoubtedly be moved and inspired by the courage and sacrifice of the men and women who sacrificed their lives for a brighter future. The D-Day Beaches leave an indelible impression, ensuring a visit that will forever resonate in memory.

2.2 Mont Saint-Michel

Scan the QR code or click on the link to Mont Saint-Michel

Mont Saint-Michel is one of Normandy and France's most iconic and impressive attractions. It is one of the most popular tourist destinations in the nation and a UNESCO World Heritage Site. Mont Saint-Michel is a medieval island abbey that rises from the sea, surrounded by a spectacular bay. It is a marvel of architecture, history, and spirituality and a must-see for travelers.

The archangel Michael first appeared to a local bishop in the eighth century, telling him to construct a sanctuary atop the mountain. This is just the beginning of the lengthy and intriguing history of Mont Saint-Michel. Since then, Mont Saint-Michel has been a place of pilgrimage, a fortress, a prison, and a cultural center. It has inspired innumerable artists, authors, and filmmakers and has withstood wars, hurricanes, fires, and revolutions.

Mont Saint-Michel is a place of wonder and beauty, where you can admire the Romanesque and Gothic abbey, the cloister, the gardens, the crypts, and the chapels. You can also explore the narrow and winding streets of the village, where you can find shops, restaurants, museums, and hotels. You can enjoy the views of the bay, the tides, and the countryside from the ramparts and the terraces.

Here are some valuable tips and details to assist you in planning your visit to Mont Saint-Michel:

Getting There: Mont Saint-Michel is approximately 220 km west of Paris and about 100 km south of Caen. You have several transportation options for your journey, including a car, train, bus, or a guided tour.

By Car: If you opt for a car, you can park at the mainland parking lot, with a daily cost of 14.50 euros. From there, you can embark on a scenic walk across the causeway, taking around 45 minutes, or catch the free shuttle bus for a quicker 15-minute ride. At the parking lot, you may also hire an electric car or a bicycle.

By Train: Travelers can take the TGV from Paris to Rennes or Dol-de-Bretagne and then board a bus to

Mont Saint-Michel. An hour and a half is how long the bus ride takes, and a whole trip ticket costs 17 euros.

By Bus: Flixbus offers bus services from Paris, Caen, or Rennes to Mont Saint-Michel. Ticket prices range between 10 and 20 euros for a one-way trip, with 3 to 5 hours of travel.

Guided Tour: A guided tour provides a convenient and comprehensive experience. Full-day or half-day trips from Paris, Caen, or Rennes include transportation, admission, and a knowledgeable guide. Prices vary depending on the provider and season, typically from 100 to 200 euros per person.

These practical insights ensure a smooth and enjoyable visit to the captivating Mont Saint-Michel, allowing you to choose the transportation that best suits your preferences and schedule.

Ideal Time to Visit:

Mont Saint-Michel welcomes visitors throughout the year, yet the optimal periods are spring or autumn. The good weather, more tolerable crowds, and a plethora of activities make for an enjoyable experience throughout these seasons.

Spring and Autumn: Visiting during spring or autumn ensures a comfortable climate, allowing you to explore without the intense summer heat. Smaller crowds contribute to a more serene ambiance, and numerous events add to the charm of your visit.

Summer: While Mont Saint-Michel remains open in the bustling summer months, the popularity can lead to substantial crowds and elevated temperatures. Expect potential queues for attractions like the abbey or shuttle bus.

Winter: Winter offers a quieter atmosphere at Mont Saint-Michel, accompanied by reduced costs. However, the weather can be chilly and damp, and certain attractions may have limited availability. It's advisable to check the opening hours and attraction prices on this [https://montsaintmicheltides.com/].

This guidance assists in planning your visit to Mont Saint-Michel, allowing you to choose a time that aligns with your preferences, whether you prioritize a vibrant atmosphere or a more tranquil experience.

What to see and do: Mont Saint-Michel offers a captivating array of experiences, with its centerpiece being the awe-inspiring abbey, a testament to Romanesque and Gothic architectural mastery. Immerse yourself in the abbey's history, symbolism, and secrets, choosing between independent exploration and guided tours. Operating hours vary, with the abbey welcoming visitors from 9:30 am to 6 pm (Usually on May to August) and 9:30 am to 5 pm (September to April). Secure your admission online in advance to skip the lines [https://www.viator.com/tours/Paris/Mont-Saint-Michel-Day-Trip-from-Paris-including-Local-Lunch/d479-2050MS]. Opting for a guided tour, an additional 3 euros expense, enriches your visit with insights lasting about an hour.

Diverse Attractions: Beyond the abbey, Mont Saint-Michel boasts several other attractions, including the Maritime and Ecology Museum, History Museum, Tiphaine's House, and the Archeoscope. These museums delve into various aspects of Mont Saint-Michel's life and history, exploring themes like tides, legends, wars, and art. Individual museum entry is 9 euros for adults and 5 euros for children, with free admission for those under 7. Consider a combined ticket for all four museums priced at 18 euros for adults, 9 euros for children, and free for children under 7.

Village Ambiance: Stroll through the village and along the ramparts to savor panoramic views, the local atmosphere, and charming shops. Purchase souvenirs, from postcards and magnets to books and regional products like biscuits, cider, or cheese. Indulge your palate at one of the restaurants, where La Mère Poulard's famous omelet or the traditional lamb of the salt marshes await.

Natural Wonders in the Bay:

1. Venture into the bay of Mont Saint-Michel, a natural wonder and biosphere reserve.
2. Witness the extraordinary tides, among the highest globally, shaping the landscape and access to the island.
3. Explore the bay's flora and fauna by walking on the sand or mud.
4. Engage in a guided walk for a safe and informative exploration of the bay's ecology and history [this website].

Mont Saint-Michel promises an enchanting blend of beauty, history, and spirituality—a place etched in your memory, beckoning you to return. It's a destination to cherish and love, offering an unforgettable travel experience.

2.3 Rouen Cathedral

Rouen Cathedral map link

Rouen Cathedral, or Cathédrale Notre-Dame de Rouen in French, stands proudly as a captivating Gothic marvel that graces the skyline of Rouen, the esteemed capital of Normandy. Serving as the ecclesiastical seat of the Archbishop of Rouen and the Primate of Normandy, this historical church ranks among France's most remarkable and revered landmarks. With over a millennium of existence, it has been a sanctuary for worship, an artistic haven, and a witness to countless events shaping the destinies of Normandy and France.

Constructed and reconstructed over more than eight centuries, from the 12th to the 16th, the cathedral boasts elements reflecting Romanesque, Gothic, and Renaissance architectural styles. Its three towers showcase distinct features: the Romanesque Tower Saint-Roman, the Gothic Tower of Butter, and the towering cast-iron spire, proudly standing as France's tallest at 151 meters. Immortalized by the renowned impressionist painter Claude Monet, the cathedral's

33

facade captures the ever-changing play of light and colors.

Step inside to discover an equally impressive interior—a soaring nave, a lavishly adorned choir, a majestic organ, and abundant stained glass windows, sculptures, and paintings. Historical people are finally laid to rest in the cathedral, including Norman dukes Rollo and Richard the Lionheart, French kings Henry II and Richard III, and the archbishops of Rouen. The Chapelle de la Vierge, or "Lady Chapel," within the cathedral houses a beautiful marble statue of the Virgin Mary and a Renaissance altar, adding to its allure.

Open to the public every day from 9 a.m. to 6 p.m. (opening at 8 am and closing at 7 pm on Sundays and public holidays), the cathedral welcomes all with free admission, though donations are appreciated. For a more enriching experience, guided tours are available at 5 euros per person, offered in French, English, and German from Monday to Saturday at 10:30 a.m, also at 2:30 p.m, and 4 pm. Reservations for tours can be made at the cathedral's front desk or online.

Nestled in the heart of Rouen on the lively Place de la Cathédrale, surrounded by shops, cafés, and restaurants, the cathedral is easily accessible by public transport. It can be reached by taxi, bike, or foot, close to various bus and metro stops, including Théâtre des Arts metro station and Cathédrale bus stop. Symbolizing the rich culture, heritage, and identity of Normandy, Rouen Cathedral invites visitors to marvel at the beauty and diversity of Gothic architecture, uncover the region's history and legends, and immerse themselves in the spiritual and artistic ambiance of this cherished Place. Whether a religious devotee, art enthusiast, or history lover, Rouen Cathedral promises inspiration and enchantment for all who visit.

2.4 Honfleur

Honfleur map link

Honfleur is an excellent choice if you seek a delightful and idyllic destination in Normandy. Nestled on the southern bank of the Seine estuary, this quaint port town is renowned for its vibrant half-timbered houses, artistic heritage, and maritime significance. For several reasons, Honfleur stands out as one of France's top tourist spots. Here's a glimpse into what you can experience in Honfleur:

1. Explore the Vieux Bassin: The old harbor steals the limelight at the heart of Honfleur. A stroll along the quays unveils the charming high, slender, timber-framed houses overlooking the dock in an array of colors. The waterfront comes alive with the bustling ambiance of cafes and restaurants, offering an opportunity to savor local delights such as seafood, cider, and Calvados. The Vieux Bassin provides an ideal vantage point to observe the ebb and flow of boats and bask in the beautiful light of the Seine estuary that has inspired countless artists.

2. Visit the Sainte-Catherine Church: This church, the biggest in France, is a remarkable marvel made of wood. Built in the fifteenth and sixteenth century by regional shipwrights, it mirrors an inverted boat due to its expert craftsmanship. The church, which has two naves and a separate bell tower, is decorated with stained glass windows, sculptures, and paintings. Admission is free daily from 9:30 am to 6 pm, with Sunday masses held at 11 am and 6 pm.

3. Discover the Art Museums: Honfleur's artistic legacy shines through at the Musée Eugène Boudin, home to a collection of works by Boudin and fellow artists.Every day except Tuesday, it is open to tourist from 10 a.m. to 12 p.m. and also from 2 p.m. to 6 p.m. Adult admission is €8, while children's admission is €4. Additionally, the Musée de la Marine, located near the Vieux Bassin, exhibits maritime history-related models, tools, and documents. Open every day except Tuesday from 10 a.m. to 12 p.m. and also from 2 p.m. to 6 p.m., Children can enter for €2, while adults must pay €4.

4. Enjoy Nature and Views: Immerse yourself in the picturesque landscapes surrounding Honfleur, accessible by foot, bike, or boat. Wander through public gardens to the beach for relaxation and recreation. See the Chapel of Notre-Dame de Grâce, which is perched on a hill and provides amazing views of the estuary and town. Built in the 17th century to honor the Virgin Mary's protection of sailors and explorers, the chapel is open daily from 9 am to 7 pm, with free admission. For a unique experience, take a boat trip from Honfleur to witness the Pont de Normandie, an impressive bridge spanning the Seine estuary. Boat trips depart from the Vieux Bassin multiple times daily, with ticket prices at €15 for adults and €10 for children.

This guide aims to inspire your visit to Honfleur, a town brimming with history, culture, and enchanting beauty. May your time in Honfleur be filled with captivating moments and cherished memories!

Chapter 3: Accommodation Options

3.1 Hotels

Hotels map directions

Normandy, a region steeped in history, culture, and natural splendor, offers a diverse array of hotels catering to various preferences and budgets, whether you're exploring the D-Day landing beaches, the iconic Mont-Saint-Michel, Impressionist sites, or the enchanting coastal towns. Among the standout accommodations is Hotel Barrière Le Normandy in Deauville, an excellent choice for those desiring a touch of the luxurious lifestyle synonymous with this renowned seaside resort.

This hotel, a splendid embodiment of Anglo-Norman architecture, envelops guests in a comfortable and lavish atmosphere. Luxuriate in the spa's amenities, indoor pool, golf course, and exceptional dining options. Positioned conveniently near the beach and city center, the hotel facilitates the exploration of Deauville and its surroundings effortlessly. Nightly rates range from $300 to $600, depending on the selected season and room type. Secure your reservation through   their website[https://www.hotelsbarriere.com/en/deauville /le-normandy.html] or by dialing +33 (0) 1 73 600 111. A stay at Hotel Barrière Le Normandy promises a luxurious and charming experience.

Hotel de Bourgtheroulde in Rouen: Nestled in the heart of Rouen, the capital of Normandy, this hotel is a captivating blend of history and elegance. Housed within a 15th-century mansion, it combines medieval and contemporary design elements seamlessly. Guests can marvel at the exquisite stained glass windows, the Gothic façade, and the Renaissance courtyard, creating a truly unique ambiance.

The hotel boasts a spa, an indoor pool, a fitness center, and a gourmet restaurant. The hotel is conveniently located within walking distance of Rouen's main attractions, including the cathedral, the Gros Horloge, and the Joan of Arc museum. It provides easy access to the city's cultural treasures. Nightly rates range from $200 to $400, varying with the season and room type. Secure   your   reservation   through   their website[https://www.hotelsparouen.com/en/] or by calling +33 2 35 14 50 50. Immerse yourself in the charm of this historic gem in the heart of Rouen.

La Ferme de la Rançonnière in Crépon: This hotel exudes charm and coziness in the serene Normandy countryside, close to the historic landing beaches. Once a 13th-century farmhouse, the establishment retains its character with stone walls, wooden beams, and inviting fireplaces. Guests can revel in the tranquility and comfort of the well-appointed rooms, lush garden, and inviting terrace. The on-site restaurant tempts the palate with delectable local cuisine crafted from fresh, organic ingredients. As an ideal hub for exploring nearby attractions such as Bayeux, Arromanches, and Omaha Beach, this hotel invites you to immerse yourself in the region's rich history. Nightly rates range from $100 to $200, contingent on the season and room type. Secure your reservation through their website[https://www.ranconniere.fr/] or by calling +33 2 31 22 21 73, and embark on a memorable journey in the heart of Normandy's picturesque countryside.

These represent just a selection of the numerous hotels available in the captivating region of Normandy. Regardless of your chosen accommodation, you are bound to experience an enchanting vacation in

Normandy—a region renowned for its extraordinary beauty and diverse offerings that showcase the essence of France.

3.2 Bed & Breakfasts

Bed and Breakfasts map directions

Normandy is a region steeped in history, culture, and natural splendor, offering diverse accommodation options for discerning travelers. In this segment, our focus is the charming realm of bed and breakfasts (B&Bs), providing a unique and intimate lodging experience.

B&Bs, distinguished by their homely ambiance, involve guests staying in private homes and relishing a homemade breakfast each morning. Typically overseen by welcoming hosts, these establishments go beyond mere lodgings, offering a personalized touch and valuable local insights. Perfect for those seeking Normandy's authentic and cozy atmosphere, B&Bs cater to a range of preferences and needs.

Normandy's B&B landscape encompasses various styles, locations, and features. Some find residence in historic edifices like castles, manors, or farmhouses, while others inhabit modern and stylish abodes. The spectrum extends to countryside retreats surrounded by verdant fields and orchards and city-centered havens close to attractions and amenities. Diverse in character, B&Bs may appeal to families, pet enthusiasts, eco-conscious travelers, or those seeking a romantic, luxurious, or quirky experience.

To assist in selecting an ideal B&B for your Normandy vacation, we've curated a list of some highly regarded establishments. We present details from reviews and feedback encompassing prices, operating hours, ratings, locations, contact information, and websites. Explore these enticing B&Bs to enhance your travel experience in Normandy.

- **La Ferme des Isles**: Nestled in the Eure department, this enchanting and rustic bed and breakfast resides within a 17th-century farmhouse. Offering four spacious and inviting rooms, each adorned with a private bathroom and a delightful garden view, the B&B provides a serene retreat. The expansive and picturesque garden invites guests to unwind amidst nature's beauty. The breakfast experience is a culinary delight, featuring fresh and organic produce from the farm—think eggs, cheese, honey, and delectable jams. Operational throughout the year, the B&B's pricing varies from 95 to 140 euros per night, contingent upon the season and chosen room. Garnering a remarkable 9.6 rating on Booking.com and boasting a coveted 5-star rating on Tripadvisor, this accommodation gem is situated in the village of Autheuil-Authouillet. Positioned approximately 30 km from Rouen and 100 km from Paris, this haven can be reached conveniently by car or train, with Gaillon-Aubevoye station merely 7 km away. For inquiries or reservations, contact the B&B at +33 06 63 46 00 45 and further details can be found on their website: (www.lafermedesisles.com).

- **Le Clos de Mondetour**: Situated in the Eure department, this refined bed and breakfast graces a 19th-century mansion, offering an exquisite and sophisticated experience. Boasting five stylish and inviting rooms, each equipped with a private bathroom and a flat-screen TV, the B&B exudes elegance. Common spaces include a lounge, library, and a charming dining room adorned with a fireplace and antique furniture, creating a cozy ambiance. Indulge in a breakfast spread that is both generous and delectable, featuring homemade pastries, bread, yogurt, and fresh fruit. Open from March to November, the B&B's nightly rates range from 120 to 160 euros, contingent upon the season and chosen room. Garnering an impressive 9.5 rating on Booking.com and proudly holding a 5-star rating on Tripadvisor, this haven is nestled in the village of Fontaine-sous-Jouy. Conveniently located about 25 km from Evreux and 80 km from Paris, reaching this delightful destination is achievable by car or train, with Bueil station a mere 4 km away. For inquiries or reservations, contact the B&B at +33 2323 668 79 and further details can be found on their website: (https://www.closdemondetour.com/en/).

- **La Maison de Lucie**: Nestled in the heart of the Calvados department, this enchanting and romantic bed and breakfast graces an 18th-century house, providing a delightful retreat. With three charming and snug rooms, each boasting a private bathroom and a captivating sea view, the B&B offers a cozy haven. Its amenities include a terrace, a garden, and a spa, inviting guests to unwind while savoring the picturesque scenery. Begin your day with a delectable breakfast in a luminous dining room featuring fresh and local products like croissants, cheese, and apple juice. Operating from April to October, the B&B's nightly rates range from 150 to 190 euros, depending on the season and chosen room. Garnering an impressive 9.4 rating on Booking.com and proudly holding a 5-star rating on Tripadvisor, this charming retreat is located in Honfleur, approximately 15 km from Deauville and 200 km from Paris. Accessing this idyllic spot is convenient, whether by car or train, to Trouville-Deauville station, 16 km away. For inquiries or reservations, contact the B&B at +33 2 31 14 40 40 and additional information can be found on their website: (www.lamaisondelucie.com).

These represent just a glimpse of the remarkable bed and breakfasts awaiting discovery in Normandy. Countless more await exploration, each boasting its distinct charm and character. To uncover a broader selection, leverage platforms such as Booking.com or Tripadvisor. Here, you can explore options, compare prices, peruse reviews, and secure your reservation. Additionally, resources like Normandy Tourism or France-Voyage provide valuable insights and tips for your Normandy adventure.

Bed and breakfasts emerge as a delightful avenue for immersing yourself in the genuine and snug ambiance of Normandy, coupled with your hosts' personal care and attention. Beyond the enriching travel experience they offer, these establishments serve as a means to bolster the local economy and culture, fostering connections with fellow travelers. Normandy accommodates whether your preference leans towards a historic, modern, rural, or urban B&B, ensuring an encounter aligned with your expectations. This discourse has provided inspiration and practical guidance for selecting the perfect B & B, setting the stage for a splendid and memorable vacation in Normandy!

3.3 Vacation Rentals

If you desire more space, privacy, and comfort than a standard hotel room, consider renting a vacation home in Normandy. These rentals cater to families, groups, or couples seeking to immerse themselves in the region's charm and authenticity. A diverse array of options, from quaint cottages and apartments to opulent villas and castles, awaits in various locations and price brackets.

Selecting a vacation rental presents several advantages:

- Economize by preparing your meals, sharing costs with fellow guests, and sidestepping additional parking, laundry, or internet access charges.

- Immerse yourself in local culture and lifestyle by residing in a typical Normandy house adorned with antiques, paintings, and books.

- Enjoy enhanced flexibility and freedom to explore the region at your own pace, unbound by hotel schedules or regulations.

- Revel in Normandy's natural beauty and tranquility, whether through a garden, terrace, or scenic views of the sea, countryside, or historic sites.

Take into consideration the following advice and suggestions to help you locate the perfect holiday property for your trip:

- Book well in advance, particularly during peak seasons (summer, holidays, festivals) or for sought-after destinations (Etretat, Honfleur, Mont-Saint-Michel).

- Rely on reputable websites or platforms such as Vacation Rentals | Normandy, Normandy Vacation Rentals | Rent By Owner™, or Normandy Vacation Rentals | Houses and More | Airbnb for browsing, comparison, and booking. Utilize filters to refine your search based on location, price, amenities, ratings, and reviews.

- Scrutinize the description, terms and conditions, and cancellation policy meticulously before confirming your booking. Ensure clarity on inclusions and exclusions, such as cleaning fees, security deposits, taxes, or additional services.

- Whenever possible, communicate directly with the owner or host to seek clarifications, confirm details, and coordinate check-in and check-out times. Don't hesitate to request local activities, sights, or dining recommendations.

- Uphold respect for the property, neighbors, and rental rules. Please treat it with the care you would your own home, leaving it as you found it. Post a review to share feedback after your stay.

Whether you seek a romantic retreat, a family escapade, or a cultural immersion, finding a vacation rental that aligns with your preferences and needs in Normandy is within reach. Your stay promises to be a memorable and authentic experience cherished for years to come. Bon voyage!

3.4 Camping

Link for camping sites

For those seeking an economical and nature-centric accommodation option in Normandy, camping is an excellent choice. Normandy boasts diverse campsites, ranging from rudimentary to opulent, catering to varied preferences. Whether you prefer setting up a tent, parking your caravan, or renting a cozy bungalow, these campsites offer a spectrum of facilities and activities to enhance your stay. Additionally, the scenic surroundings invite exploration, allowing you to delve into the beauty and history of Normandy. Below, discover some of the finest campsites in Normandy, carefully selected based on their location, pricing, and ratings.

La Vallée: This distinguished campsite in the enchanting coastal town of Houlgate on the Côte Fleurie holds a prestigious 5-star rating. Nestled in a lush valley, surrounded by hills and woods, it provides a serene environment near the beach. The campsite offers upscale accommodations and indulgent amenities, including a heated indoor pool, a spa, a restaurant, and a kids' club. Various lodging options are available, ranging from tents and caravans to mobile homes and cottages. Nightly rates vary from 25 euros to 200 euros, contingent on the season and the chosen accommodation type. From April to October, reservations can be conveniently made through this website. With a commendable rating of 3.9 out of 5, based on 1332 reviews, this campsite ensures a luxurious and highly-rated experience.

Le Fanal: This 4-star campsite is situated in Isigny-sur-Mer, a quaint town on the Cotentin Peninsula, near the banks of the Vire River and the historic D-Day beaches. The campsite ensures a pleasant stay with comfortable accommodations and welcoming services, featuring amenities like a heated outdoor pool, a playground, a bar, and a grocery store. Diverse lodging options allow guests to choose from tents, caravans, chalets, or lodges. Nightly rates vary from 15 euros to 100 euros, depending on the season and the selected accommodation type. From April to September, reservations can be conveniently made through their website[https://www.pascal-borrell.com/fr/]. With a commendable rating of 4.1 out of 5, based on 367 reviews, this campsite promises a delightful and well-reviewed experience.

Les Castels Château de Martragny: This 4-star campsite, nestled in Martragny, a village near Bayeux, is gracefully situated within the grounds of an 18th-century château, exuding a romantic and elegant ambiance. The campsite provides spacious and well-appointed accommodations and top-notch services, including a heated outdoor pool, a tennis court, a restaurant, and a library. Guests can choose from various lodgings, such as tents, caravans, gîtes, or rooms within the château. Nightly rates span from 20 euros to 150 euros, contingent on the season and the chosen accommodation type. From May to September, reservations can be conveniently made online through [https://www.les-castels.co.uk/camping/les-castels-chateau-de-martragny]. With an impressive rating of 4.3 out of 5, based on 246 reviews, this campsite ensures a delightful and highly rated experience for its visitors.

Huttopia Les Falaises: This 3-star campsite, nestled in Saint-Pierre-en-Port, a village on the Alabaster Coast, gracefully sits atop the cliffs, providing a mesmerizing sea vista and creating a tranquil setting. The campsite offers unpretentious and comfortable accommodations, complemented by eco-friendly amenities, including a natural pool, a snack bar, a bike rental, and a yoga class. Accommodation options range from tents, caravans, and cabins to tipis, with prices varying from 15 euros to 80 euros per night, depending on the season and chosen lodging type. Open from April to October, reservations can be conveniently made online through [https://europe.huttopia.com/en/site/les-falaises-normandy/]. Garnering an impressive rating of 4.4 out of 5 from 153 reviews, this campsite promises its guests a serene and highly-rated experience.

Embracing camping presents an enjoyable and cost-effective way to immerse yourself in the nature and culture of Normandy. Discovering a campsite that aligns with your preferences and budget ensures a memorable experience. Beyond its economic appeal, camping fosters connections with fellow travelers and locals, providing opportunities to exchange stories and valuable tips. Engaging in camping becomes a pathway to live out the adventure Normandy offers.

Chapter 4: Dining and Cuisine

4.1 Normandy's Specialties

Normandy is a region of France that boasts a rich and diverse culinary heritage, influenced by its coastal and rural landscapes, history and culture, and proximity to England. Normandy is famous for its dairy products, especially its cheeses and creams, its apples and pears, which are used to make delicious drinks and desserts, and its seafood, which is abundant and varied. Whether looking for a hearty meal, a light snack, or a sweet treat, you will find something to satisfy your taste buds in Normandy. Here are some specialties you should notice when visiting this gastronomic paradise.

Escalope Normande: This delightful dish is a harmonious blend of flavors, featuring a veal escalope—a thin, succulent slice of meat—simmered in a velvety sauce enriched with mushrooms, butter, and occasionally a touch of Calvados, an exquisite apple brandy. Typically accompanied by rice, potatoes, or pasta, it offers a wonderful opportunity to relish the luscious and smooth essence of Normandy cream.

Marmite Dieppoise: This flavorsome seafood medley originated in the maritime hub of Dieppe, where skilled fishermen would concoct a savory stew using their daily catch. Cooked in a large pot, or "marmite," this delectable creation features a blend of cider, cream, butter, and herbs. The stew showcases diverse fish, including cod, haddock, monkfish, sole, and shellfish such as mussels, clams, and prawns. A comforting and robust dish, it highlights the freshness and variety of seafood found in the bountiful waters of Normandy.

Tripes à la mode de Caen: This dish, not universally appealing but a delicacy for the adventurous palate, involves simmering the stomach, feet, and bones of a cow for hours in a broth enriched with vegetables, garlic, peppercorns, cider, and Calvados. This culinary tradition in Normandy dates back to the Middle Ages, resulting in a tender and flavorful creation. Legend has it that William the Conqueror, the Duke of Normandy who later became the King of England, was an enthusiast for this dish.

Trou Normand: This practice, not classified as a dish but a ritual, is observed between courses or as a dessert. It involves a small glass of Calvados poured over a scoop of apple sorbet. The intention is to refresh the palate, facilitate digestion, and arouse the appetite. The delightful contrast between the cold and tangy sorbet and the warm and robust Calvados creates an enticing experience that leaves you eager for more.

Omelette à la Mère Poulard: This renowned omelet is a specialty served at the Mère Poulard Inn in the iconic Mont Saint-Michel. The omelet is celebrated for its light and fluffy texture, achieved by vigorously whisking the eggs in a copper bowl and cooking them over high heat in a spacious skillet. Whether enjoyed plain or filled with ingredients like cheese, ham, mushrooms, or others, it is a straightforward yet gratifying dish that has captivated numerous celebrities and visitors.

Barfleur mussels: Barfleur is a quaint fishing village that hosts France's largest reserve of wild mussels. These mussels have distinct taste and quality and are nurtured in pure and nutrient-rich waters. They are served alongside fries or bread and are typically prepared in a white wine sauce featuring garlic, parsley, and cream. A culinary delight for seafood enthusiasts, these mussels can be savored at one of the many restaurants lining the harbor.

Honfleur grey shrimp: Honfleur stands as another enchanting fishing port renowned for its grey shrimp, often called the "queen of the estuary." Despite their small size, these shrimp boast a prized sweet and delicate flavor. Frequently enjoyed as an appetizer, they are meticulously hand-peeled and paired with buttered bread. Additionally, they play a versatile role in creating soups, salads, or quiches.

Lapin à la Havraise: This represents a rabbit delicacy distinctive to Le Havre, a significant maritime and industrial center. The rabbit undergoes marination in cider and Calvados, subsequently cooked with onions, carrots, bacon, and cream. It is a robust and flavorful dish, embodying the city's character and historical significance.

These represent just a selection of the culinary delights waiting to be discovered in Normandy, a region that caters abundantly to enthusiasts of fine cuisine. Normandy's gastronomy seamlessly blends tradition, innovation, simplicity, and sophistication, drawing inspiration from its fertile lands and bountiful seas. It's a culinary experience that promises to astonish, bring joy, and leave you yearning for more.

4.2 Top Restaurants

Map direction link to top restaurants in Normandy

Normandy is famous for its rich and varied cuisine, influenced by its maritime location, agricultural heritage, and historical ties with neighboring regions and countries. Whether you crave fresh seafood, creamy cheeses, succulent meats, or indulgent pastries, you will find something to satisfy your taste buds in Normandy's top restaurants. According to our expert reviewers and local insiders, here are some of the best places to eat in Normandy.

Le Catleya (Honfleur): This distinguished restaurant, adorned with a Michelin star, presents an exquisite and innovative culinary journey, highlighting the finest offerings from Normandy's rich agricultural and culinary heritage. Chef Jérôme Bansard crafts seasonal menus that marry traditional French culinary techniques with contemporary flair, featuring delectable dishes like scallops with black truffle, duck foie gras paired with apple and ginger, or lamb complemented by rosemary and garlic. The dining ambiance exudes elegance, providing captivating views of Honfleur's charming harbor, and the service is impeccably attentive. Prices for a three-course menu range from €55 to €95, and reservations are indispensable. Operating from Wednesday to Sunday, with service hours from 12:00 to 13:30 and 19:00 to 21:00. For reservations, contact +33 2 31 89 18 19; more information can be found on this website.

L'Atelier du Goût (Caen): If you seek a warm and laid-back venue to savor genuine Normandy cuisine, L'Atelier du Goût is the perfect choice. This restaurant, run by a welcoming family, offers hearty and flavorsome dishes like chicken infused with cider and cream, pork accompanied by camembert cheese, or an apple tart enhanced with Calvados. Portions are ample, prices remain reasonable, and the ambiance exudes a friendly, easygoing atmosphere. Additionally, you can purchase some of the locally sourced products featured in their kitchen, including cheeses, ciders, jams, and honey. Main course prices range from €15 to €25, and reservations are advisable. Operating from Monday to Saturday, with service hours from 12:00 to 14:00 and 19:00 to 22:00. For reservations, contact +33 164 69 19 21; further details can be found on their website[https://latelier-du-gout-84.webself.net/].

Le Moulin de Jean (Cuves): For an intimate and rural setting, visit Le Moulin de Jean, a former watermill transformed into an enchanting restaurant and hotel. The menu showcases local delights, such as oysters from Saint-Vaast-la-Hougue, veal from Cotentin, or cheese from Livarot. The dishes are artfully presented, bursting with flavors, and complemented by an extensive and thoughtfully curated wine list. Guests can opt for the snug dining room or the terrace with views of the river and garden. Prices for a three-course menu range from €39 to €75, and reservations are essential. Operating from Tuesday to Sunday, with service hours from 12:15 to 13:45 and 19:15 to 21:15. To reserve your spot, contact +33 2 33 48 39 29.

Restaurant la Table d'Hôtes (Bayeux): Situated in the heart of Bayeux, a town renowned for its historic tapestry and cathedral, this restaurant is curated by Chef Stéphane Carbone, a proud Normandy native championing local and organic produce. Chef Carbone crafts inventive and seasonal delicacies, such as lobster paired with green asparagus, beef accompanied by morel mushrooms, or strawberry infused with basil and lemon. The dining ambiance is contemporary and understated, complemented by attentive and professional service. Menu prices range from €39 to €69 for a three-course experience, and reservations are recommended. Operating from Tuesday to Saturday, with service hours from 12:00 to 13:30 and 19:00 to 21:30. For reservations or further inquiries, contact +33 2 31 97 18 44.

Aroma (Rouen): If you're seeking a unique culinary experience, consider Aroma, a fusion restaurant harmonizing French and Mediterranean flavors. Executive Chef David Goerne employs fresh, high-quality ingredients to craft vibrant, flavorful, and inventive dishes. Delight your palate with offerings like tuna tataki with sesame and soy, lamb tagine accompanied by couscous and dried fruits, or chocolate cake infused with orange and cardamom. A wine bar within the restaurant offers the perfect setting to enjoy a glass of wine and delectable tapas. Main course prices range from €18 to €32, and reservations are recommended. Aroma welcomes guests from Tuesday to Saturday, with service hours from 12:00 to 14:00 and 19:00 to 22:00.

Whether you seek a refined dining experience, a quaint restaurant, or an innovative fusion eatery, Normandy has a diverse culinary scene to explore. While the mentioned restaurants offer exceptional choices, the region boasts numerous hidden gems to uncover and savor.

4.3 Local Markets

Exploring Normandy's culinary treasures is best done through a visit to its local markets, where an abundance of fresh, seasonal, and organic products awaits. Whether your cravings lean towards cheese, cider, seafood, meat, fruits, vegetables, or pastries, the vibrant stalls offer a feast for the senses. Engaging with the amiable vendors adds a personal touch as they eagerly share their stories and recipes. Below are some of Normandy's enchanting and well-regarded markets, according to reviews and ratings from fellow travelers.

Caen: Normandy's capital boasts two prominent markets held on Sunday mornings. Along the marina, the larger one showcases an array of fish, shellfish, cheese, bread, and flowers. Meanwhile, the smaller market on Place Saint-Sauveur, surrounded by 18th-century buildings, features local specialties like cider, calvados, andouille, and camembert. Both markets, open from 8 am to 1 pm, are conveniently located within walking distance of the city center and its attractions.

Honfleur: Renowned for its wooden church, art galleries, and seafood restaurants, Honfleur hosts a delightful market on Saturday mornings throughout the year and on Wednesday mornings from April to

October. Centered around the church of Sainte-Catherine and its belfry tower, this market offers an extensive selection, including cheese, honey, jam, crepes, cider, and calvados. The Wednesday market features organic and bioproducts, local crafts, and souvenirs. Operating from 8 am to 1 pm, the market is situated near the harbor and the old town.

Cherbourg: Serving as the gateway to the Cotentin Peninsula, Cherbourg charms with its natural beauty and historical heritage. The city hosts various markets, predominantly on Thursdays and Sundays, at locations like Place de Gaulle and Place Centrale and in front of the main post office. These markets provide diverse offerings, from fish, seafood, and cheese to fruits, vegetables, and flowers. Additionally, the first Saturday of each month sees a flea market near the Basilica of Sainte-Trinité, perfect for hunting antiques, books, and collectibles. Operating from 8 am to 1 pm, these markets are conveniently located near the city center and its attractions.

Whichever market you explore, a visit promises an authentic taste of Normandy's diverse and delightful flavors, making it one of France's most captivating regions.

Chapter 5: Things to Do and Outdoor Activities

5.1 Hiking Trails

Link to Hiking Trails

Normandy is a region that offers a variety of landscapes and scenery for hiking enthusiasts. Whether you prefer the coast, the countryside, or the forest, you can find a hiking trail that suits your level and interest. Normandy has more than 3,000 km of long-distance hiking trails, also known as GR (Grande Randonnée) routes, that link the region with the rest of France and Europe. You can also choose from many shorter and circular trails called PR (Promenade et Randonnée) routes to explore the local attractions and heritage. In this subtopic, we will introduce you to some of the best hiking trails in Normandy.

The Bay of Mont-Saint-Michel Trail: Embark on one of Normandy's most iconic and breathtaking hiking trails. This remarkable journey allows you to traverse the bay of Mont-Saint-Michel on foot, offering awe-inspiring views of this UNESCO World Heritage Site. Spanning approximately 7 km, the trail unfolds over a leisurely 3-hour duration. While not a strenuous hike, it necessitates careful considerations, including checking tide times, donning suitable footwear and attire, and following a certified guide for a safe experience. Accessible from April to October, this extraordinary trail is priced at 10 euros per person. Bookings can be conveniently made online or at the tourist office in Genêts, serving as the trail's starting point. To commence your adventure, contact the tourist office at +33 2 33 48 81 00. Immerse yourself in the captivating beauty of Mont-Saint-Michel's Bay through this unforgettable hiking experience.

The Alabaster Coast Trail: Embark on a picturesque and refreshing hiking trail tracing the cliffs of the Alabaster Coast in Seine-Maritime, forming part of the extensive GR 21 route spanning from Le Havre to Le Tréport, covering a remarkable 190 km. Whether you opt for the entire route or select a specific section, the journey promises breathtaking views of the sea, the iconic white chalk cliffs, and charming seaside towns like Etretat, Fécamp, and Dieppe. This trail, accessible throughout the year, offers varying difficulty levels contingent on the terrain and weather conditions. For comprehensive information and maps, visit the Seine-

Maritime Tourism Board's website at www.seine-maritime-tourisme.com. Immerse yourself in the beauty of the Alabaster Coast, where every step unfolds a new chapter of scenic wonders.

The Suisse Normande Trail: Embark on a captivating and diverse hiking adventure exploring the Suisse Normande, an undulating and forested region reminiscent of Switzerland. This trail forms part of the GR 36 route, spanning the length of Normandy from north to south, encompassing a total distance of 320 km. Whether you opt for the entire route or select a specific segment, the journey unfolds the natural and cultural wonders of Suisse Normande, featuring rocky crags, deep gorges, medieval castles, and charming villages. Accessible year-round, the trail offers varying difficulty levels, from easy to challenging, dictated by elevation changes and distances covered. For detailed information and maps, visit the Calvados Tourism Board website at www.calvados-tourisme.co.uk. Immerse yourself in the allure of Suisse Normande, where every step brings you closer to the region's enchanting landscapes and rich history.

Explore the wealth of incredible hiking trails that Normandy has to offer, each boasting its distinct charm and personality. Uncover more options and plan your adventure using the Normandy

Tourism[https://en.normandie-tourisme.fr/], where you can compare ratings, read reviews, and create your itinerary. Local tourist offices are also valuable resources for obtaining maps and trail suggestions.

When hiking in Normandy, meticulous planning is crucial. Ensure you have a well-thought-out route, bring a map and a mobile phone, wear sturdy walking shoes, and carry ample water and snacks. Above all, show utmost respect for nature and the environment.

Hiking presents an excellent opportunity to immerse yourself in Normandy's authentic and diverse beauty while relishing the fresh air and exercise. It's also a fantastic way to connect with fellow nature enthusiasts and share your passion for adventure. Whether you prefer a leisurely stroll, extensive trek, coastal exploration, or forest immersion, Normandy offers a hiking trail perfectly suited to your preferences and expectations.

May this information inspire and guide you as you choose the ideal hiking trail for your Normandy adventure. Wishing you a remarkable and memorable hiking experience in the stunning landscapes of Normandy!

5.2 Water Sports

Link to water sports locations

Normandy, a haven for water sports enthusiasts, boasts 600 km of coastline, sun-drenched seascapes, and abundant lakes, rivers, and waterways. Whether you seek adrenaline, fun, or relaxation, many options await, catering to various tastes and skill levels. Dive into sailing, surfing, kite-surfing, sand yachting, canoeing, kayaking, wakeboarding, stand-up paddleboarding, and more.

Discover some of the prime water sports spots in Normandy:

1. Cercle Nautique Villers-sur-Mer: Nestled in the charming seaside resort of Villers-sur-Mer, this sailing club offers courses, rentals, and exciting events. From catamarans and dinghies to windsurfs and paddle boards, a range of options awaits. Operating from Monday to Sunday, 9 am to 5 pm (season-dependent), prices vary based on activity and duration. For instance, a one-hour catamaran rental costs €35 for one person. Reach the club by car, train, or bus from Caen or Deauville. Contact: 02 31 87 00 30, [Cercle Nautique Villers-sur-Mer](https://www.normandie-seine-estuaire.fr/que-faire-dans-lestuaire/nautisme/centres-nautiques/cercle-nautique-de-villers-sur-mer-2/).

2. Club de Plongée de Trouville sur Mer: Ideal for both novices and experienced divers, this diving club allows exploration of the underwater wonders along the Normandy coast. Discover wrecks, reefs, caves, and marine life in the English Channel with equipment, training, and expert guidance. Open Monday and Thursday, 8 pm to 9:30 pm, prices vary by diving type and level. Find the club on Boulevard Cahotte, Trouville sur Mer. Accessible by car, train, or bus from Caen or Le Havre. Contact: +33 652187997, [Club de Plongée de Trouville sur Mer](https://www.club-plongee-trouville.fr/).

3. Cabourg Jet: This jet ski center, located in the chic resort of Cabourg, offers thrilling rides along the Normandy coast. Opt for solo or duo jet skis with or without a guide, or experience the excitement of flyboarding. Open daily starting from 9 am to 8 pm, prices range from €70 to €180 for jet ski rentals and €80 to €150 for flyboard sessions. Visit the center on

Avenue Durand Morimbau. Accessible by car, train, or bus from Caen or Lisieux. Contact: 06 74 44 92 59, [Cabourg Jet](https://cabourg-jet.com/).

These are just a glimpse of the water sports opportunities in Normandy. Explore more Normandy Tourism, Tripadvisor, and Watersports options on the Normandy websites. Whatever you choose, expect an exhilarating and unforgettable experience in Normandy.

5.3 Cycling Routes

Link to the Cycling Routes

Normandy is a haven for cyclists, offering diverse routes catering to various levels and interests. Cyclists can traverse coastal paths, countryside lanes, or city circuits, immersing themselves in the beauty and history of this enchanting region. The journey also presents opportunities to savor local cuisine, embrace the culture, and experience the warm hospitality of Normandy.

Several cycling routes beckon, accommodating different preferences and timeframes:

1. **The Vélomaritime:** Embark on this extensive cycling journey tracing Normandy's coastline from Le Tréport to Mont Saint-Michel. Forming part of EuroVelo 4, which links Roscoff in Brittany to Kiev in Ukraine, the Vélomaritime spans around 500 km in Normandy. The route encompasses picturesque locales such as the Alabaster Coast, Côte Fleurie, D-Day Beaches, and the Bay of Mont Saint-Michel. With mostly flat terrain and clear signposts, the route offers various accommodation and service options. Cyclists

can complete the entire route in approximately ten days or opt for a shorter section. [More information](https://www.velomaritime.com/).

2. The Véloscénie: Connecting Paris to Mont Saint-Michel, this mid-distance cycling route spans 450 km, traversing four regions and three natural parks. Offering a diverse experience, the Véloscénie takes cyclists from the urban and cultural allure of Paris to the rural landscapes of Normandy. The route, characterized by hills, utilizes greenways, cycle paths, and small roads. Along the way, cyclists encounter historical and cultural landmarks, including Notre-Dame Cathedral, Chartres Cathedral, Château de Maintenon, and Château de Carrouges. The full route can be completed in about seven days, or cyclists can choose a shorter section. [More information](https://www.veloscenie.com/).

3. The Tour de Manche: A circular route encircling the English Channel, the Tour de Manche covers approximately 1200 km, weaving through Normandy, Brittany, and England. The varied and challenging route utilizes greenways, cycle paths, and roads showcasing maritime and cultural heritage. Highlights along the way include the Jurassic Coast, Dartmoor National Park, Pink Granite Coast, Cap Fréhel, and Mont Saint-Michel. Cyclists can complete the entire route in about 15 days or select a shorter section that suits their schedule.

Cycling in Normandy provides a delightful and healthy means to explore its nature and culture. Cyclists can choose routes matching their skill levels and interests, creating memorable adventures. Guided tours or bike rentals are also available for those who prefer organized excursions. [More information](https://www.normandie-tourisme.fr/cycling-in-normandy).

Cycling enables individuals to uncover Normandy's hidden gems at their own pace, connecting with the wind, sun, and sea and living the dream of Normandy.

Chapter 6: Art, Culture, and Entertainment

6.1 Museums

Normandy, a region steeped in France's rich and diverse artistic, cultural, and historical heritage, boasts many museums catering to varied interests. Whether your fascination lies in paintings, sculptures, ceramics, tapestries, or the region's history—from Viking invasions to the D-Day landings—Normandy offers museums that cater to every taste and curiosity. Here are some must-visit museums that encapsulate the fascinating essence of this region:

<u>**Link to Mémorial de Caen direction**</u>

1. Mémorial de Caen: A comprehensive and remarkable museum dedicated to World War II, the Mémorial de Caen stands among the most extensive globally. Situated on the grounds of a former German bunker, In addition to studying the D-Day events and the Battle of Normandy, the museum also looks at the origins, effects, and international resistance movements of the war, genocide, mass violence, and the subsequent liberation and reconstruction of Europe. With its enormous collection of relics, records, images, films, and testimonies, the museum offers a deep insight into the effects of the conflict. Additionally, visitors can explore a movie theater, a gift shop, and three gardens honoring soldiers from the United States, Canada, and Britain.

 **Link to Musée Nicolas Poussin**

2. Musée Nicolas Poussin: Nestled in the picturesque town of Les Andelys along the Seine, the Musée Nicolas Poussin is a charming repository showcasing the works of Nicolas Poussin, a prominent painter of the 17th-century French classical school. Housed in a former episcopal palace, the museum displays a collection of paintings, drawings, engravings, sculptures, and local archaeological and historical artifacts. The museum offers a splendid view of the Seine and the medieval fortress Château Gaillard, built by Richard the Lionheart.

Link to Musée des Beaux-Arts de Rouen direction

3. Musée des Beaux-Arts de Rouen: In the heart of Rouen, the capital of Normandy, the Musée des Beaux-Arts de Rouen is renowned as one of France's finest art museums. With a collection exceeding 8,000 works spanning the 15th to the 21st centuries, the museum occupies a majestic building partially designed by Napoleon III. It houses masterpieces by celebrated artists like Caravaggio, Rubens, Velázquez, Delacroix, Renoir, Monet, Degas, Sisley, Gauguin, Picasso, and Duchamp. Notably, the museum features a dedicated section to the Impressionist movement, born in Normandy, showcasing Monet's famous paintings of Rouen Cathedral.

Link to Musée du Débarquement Utah

4. Musée du Débarquement Utah Beach: Commemorating the D-Day landings on June 6, 1944, at Utah Beach, this museum is housed in a former German bunker captured by American troops. Displaying uniforms, weapons, vehicles, and personal items belonging to the soldiers involved in the operation, the museum also features a rare B-26 bomber, one of only six remaining worldwide. A cinema within the museum presents a documentary on the historic landings.

Link to Musée de la Tapisserie de Bayeux

5. Musée de la Tapisserie de Bayeux: This historical treasure trove of a museum features the Bayeux Tapestry, a medieval masterwork that depicts the Norman conquest of England in 1066. The tapestry, measuring about 70 meters in length and 50 centimeters in height, narrates 58 scenes of the Battle of Hastings, William the Conqueror's coronation, and the events leading up to them. Accompanied by a Latin commentary, the tapestry has been preserved for over 900 years, offering a captivating journey into medieval art and history.

Normandy's museums are not just repositories of knowledge but also evoke beauty and emotion. They allow visitors to appreciate the works of great artists, witness pivotal historical events, and explore the traditions and identities of the region's inhabitants. Whether your interests lie in art, history, or the lives of famous personalities like Claude Monet, Gustave Flaubert, or Victor Hugo, Normandy's museums cater to various tastes and curiosities.

6.2 Art Galleries

Link Art Galleries direction

Normandy is not just a haven of history and nature but also a captivating realm of art and culture. The region, particularly beloved by the Impressionists, has been a muse for artists who sought to capture the ever-changing light, hues of landscapes, seas, and the essence of its people. Immerse yourself in the artistic tapestry of Normandy by exploring some of the finest art galleries:

1. Galeries Bartoux Normandy (Honfleur): Located in the heart of Honfleur near the Sainte-Catherine Church, this gallery showcases contemporary artists hailing from France and beyond. From the vibrant works of Robert Combas and JonOne to the expressive pieces of Philippe Pasqua and Richard Orlinski, the gallery presents a diverse array of paintings, sculptures, and prints. Open daily starting from 10 am to 7 pm, admission is free.

2. L'Atelier du Goût (Caen): More than just an art gallery, L'Atelier du Goût offers a unique fusion of art and culinary delights. This gallery, run by a creative couple of artists and chefs, tantalizes the visual and gustatory senses. Delight in edible artworks such as cakes, pastries, chocolates, and jams crafted from local and organic ingredients. Admission is free Monday to Saturday from 10 am to 7 pm.

3. Le Moulin de Jean (Cuves): Nestled in a former watermill surrounded by a picturesque garden and a river, this gallery showcases the watercolors of local painter Jean-Pierre Leclerc. With scenes and landscapes capturing the essence of Normandy infused with poetry and humor, the gallery also offers a hotel with comfortable rooms and a gourmet restaurant. Open Tuesday to Sunday starting from 10 am to 6 pm, admission is free.

4. Restaurant la Table d'Hôtes (Bayeux): Situated in the heart of Bayeux, this gallery cum restaurant provides a unique dining experience amid the works of Stéphane Carbone. A fervent advocate of local and organic products, Carbone's colorful and expressive paintings reflect his passion for nature and food. Open Tuesday to Saturday starting from 12 pm to 2 pm aslo from 7 pm to 10 pm, admission is free.

5. Aroma (Rouen): A delightful fusion of art and cuisine, Aroma blends French and Mediterranean influences. Displaying the works of painter David Goerne, inspired by culinary experiments and travels, the gallery features vibrant colors and geometric shapes. With a wine bar offering a selection of wines and tapas, Aroma is open Tuesday to Saturday which starts from 12 pm to 2 pm and also from 7 pm to 10 pm, with free admission.

Whether seeking traditional or modern art galleries, Normandy offers diverse options. These highlighted galleries represent just a glimpse into this captivating region's rich art and cultural scene. Set off on a voyage to discover and admire the artistic gems of Normandy!

6.3 Music and Festivals

Normandy isn't just a tapestry of history and nature; it resonates with the harmonies of music and the vibrancy of festivals. Throughout the year, this region pulsates with events celebrating its diverse musical landscape, ranging from classical to rock, jazz to folk, opera to electro. Beyond the melodies, you can immerse yourself in the festive spirit of Normandy's traditional events, including carnivals, fairs, and commemorations. Here are some standout music and festivals that capture the essence of Normandy:

1. The D-Day Festival honors the historic 1944 Battle of Normandy and the D-Day Landings, this festival spans from June 1 to 16, 2024, unfolding across iconic locations like Caen, Bayeux, Arromanches, and Omaha Beach. With over 100 events encompassing parachuting, parades, concerts, historical re-enactments, fireworks, exhibitions, and projections, the festival is a poignant tribute to the Allied soldiers and the resilient Normans. Free and open to all, it profoundly honors the pursuit of freedom and peace.

2. The Deauville American Film Festival: Renowned as one of Europe's premier film festivals, this event, taking place from September 6 to 15, 2024, in the elegant Deauville resort, celebrates the richness and

originality of American cinema. The festival transforms Deauville into a cinematic haven with over 100 film screenings, ranging from Hollywood blockbusters to independent treasures, competitions, tributes, masterclasses, and interactions with actors and directors. Drawing film enthusiasts and celebrities alike, it's a unique opportunity to delve into the best of American cinema.

3. The Tall Ships' Races: A breathtaking spectacle, The Tall Ships' Races gathers some of the world's most majestic sailing vessels for a joyous competition. In 2025, commencing from Le Havre, From July 4 to 7, the biggest port in Normandy and a World Heritage Site by UNESCO will be the scene of this event. The free and open event invites admiration for the beauty and skill of these maritime vessels and their crews, featuring a mesmerizing parade of sail, a race village, concerts, fireworks, and family-friendly activities.

Whichever event you choose, your time in Normandy promises to be an unforgettable experience in one of France's most dynamic and diverse regions.

Chapter 7: 7-Day Itinerary

7.1 Day 1: Arrival and Exploring Caen

Welcome to Caen, the heartbeat of Lower Normandy and a city steeped in history, culture, and natural wonders. As you embark on your first day, immerse yourself in the tapestry of Caen's past, where echoes of William the Conqueror and World War II resonate. Here's a curated itinerary to unveil the charms of this captivating city:

Begin your day at the Mémorial de Caen:

Explore the Mémorial de Caen, a poignant museum memorializing the 20th century, particularly World War II and the D-Day Landings. The immersive exhibits delve into the war's causes, consequences, and aftermath, emphasizing themes of peace, reconciliation, and human rights. Visit the original bunker where General Wilhelm Richter orchestrated the defense of Normandy's beaches on D-Day. Open from 9 am to 6 pm (February to December) and 9:30 am to 7 pm (July and August), admission is 19.80 euros for adults and 16.50 euros for students and seniors. Book your tickets [online](www.memorial-caen.fr) or on-site.

Next, explore the Abbaye aux Hommes:

Visit the magnificent Abbaye aux Hommes, a Romanesque abbey established in the eleventh century by William the Conqueror. This abbey, his final resting place, showcases the exquisite Norman architecture of the Saint-Etienne church, adorned with elegant columns and impressive vaults. Wander through the cloister and former monastic buildings, now housing the city hall and the Museum of Normandy. Open from 9:30 am to 12:30 pm and 2 pm to 6 pm (April to September) and 10 am to 12:30 pm and 2 pm to 5 pm (October to March), admission is 5.50 euros for adults and 3.50 euros for students and seniors. Secure your tickets [online](www.abbayeauxhommes.com) or at the entrance.

Lunch at Quartier du Vaugueux:

Head to Quartier du Vaugueux for a historical and lively dining experience. Amid narrow cobblestone streets and medieval charm, relish local specialties like tripe à la mode de Caen, andouille de Vire, or teurgoule (a rice pudding). Recommended restaurants include Le P'tit Vaugueux, La Cour Anteol, and Le Bistrot Basque, with prices ranging from 15 to 30 euros per person. Reserve a table [online](www.restaurantname.com) or walk in for a delightful culinary journey.

Afternoon exploration at the Château de Caen:

Continue your journey at the Château de Caen, a medieval fortress crafted by William the Conqueror in the 11th century. One of Europe's largest and oldest castles, it offers panoramic city and countryside views. Stroll along the ramparts, explore the remains of the great hall and chapel, and visit the Musée des Beaux-Arts and Musée de Normandie within the castle. Open from 9:30 am to 6 pm (April to September) and 10 am to 5 pm (October to March), admission is 5.50 euros for adults and 3.50 euros for students and seniors. Book tickets [online](www.chateau.caen.fr) or on-site.

Conclude your day with a serene stroll in La Colline aux Oiseaux:

Wind down your day at La Colline aux Oiseaux, a park and garden born from a former landfill. Covering 17 hectares, it features thematic gardens, a mini-farm, a playground, and a pond. Home to diverse birds and animals, the park is open from 8 am to 8 pm (April to September) and 8 am to 6 pm (October to March). Admission is free. Access the park by bus, tram, or car. For inquiries, contact +33 2 31 30 48 38 or visit www.lacollineauxoiseaux.fr.

Retreat to your hotel or venture into Caen's vibrant evening scene as the day concludes. Tomorrow, your exploration continues with the D-Day Landing Beaches and the American Cemetery. Stay tuned for the next chapter of this guide, guiding you through your second day in Normandy.

7.2 Day 2: D-Day Beaches

Embark on the second day of your Normandy journey, delving into the pivotal moments of the 20th century—the D-Day landings on June 6, 1944. Explore the hallowed grounds where Allied forces initiated the liberation of France and Europe from Nazi occupation: Utah, Omaha, Gold, Juno, and Sword beaches. Witness the remnants of the artificial harbor at Arromanches, the imposing cliffs at Pointe du Hoc, and the poignant cemeteries and memorials honoring the fallen heroes. Maximize your day by starting early and following this recommended route:

Utah Beach:

Commence your day at Utah Beach, the westernmost and least fortified of the D-Day beaches. The U.S. 4th Infantry Division landed here with comparatively fewer casualties. Immerse yourself in the history and challenges of the operation at the Utah Beach D-Day Museum, housed in a former German bunker. Open daily from 9:30 am to 6 pm (or 7 pm from April to September), admission is €9.50 for adults, €6.50 for children, and €8.50 for students and seniors. The museum is located at Sainte-Marie-du-Mont, accessible by car from Bayeux in about an hour. Contact: 02 33 71 53 35, [Utah Beach D-Day Museum](www.utah-beach.com).

Pointe du Hoc:

Proceed to Pointe du Hoc, a strategic promontory between Utah and Omaha beaches. U.S. Army Rangers scaled the 100-foot cliffs under enemy fire to secure the position. Explore craters, bunkers, and gun emplacements that bear witness to the intensity of the assault. Visit the Pointe du Hoc Visitor Center, showcasing exhibits, films, and artifacts related to the mission. Open daily from 9 am to 6 pm (or 5 pm from October to March), admission is free. The visitor center is reachable by car from Utah Beach in about 20 minutes. Contact: 02 31 22 45 80, [Pointe du Hoc Visitor Center](www.pointeduhoc.org).

Omaha Beach:

Move to Omaha Beach, the bloodiest and most renowned of the D-Day beaches, where the U.S. 1st and 29th Infantry Divisions faced fierce German resistance. Walk along the four-mile stretch of sand, contemplating the courage and sacrifice of the soldiers. Visit the Omaha Beach Memorial Museum, displaying a collection of uniforms, weapons, vehicles, and personal items from the landing. Open daily from 9:30 am to 6:30 pm (or 7 pm from April to September), admission is €8.50 for adults, €5.50 for children, and €7.50 for students and seniors. The museum is situated at Saint-Laurent-sur-Mer, accessible by car from

Pointe du Hoc in about 15 minutes. Contact: 02 31 21 97 44, [Omaha Beach Memorial Museum](www.omahabeach-memorial.org).

Normandy American Cemetery and Memorial:

Honor the 9,387 American servicemen buried in the Normandy American Cemetery, which has a commanding view of Omaha Beach. Walk among the rows of white marble crosses and stars of David. Explore the memorial, chapel, garden of the missing, and the visitor center narrating the American involvement in World War II. Open daily from 9 am to 6 pm (or 5 pm from October to March), admission is free. The cemetery and visitor center are reachable by car from the beach in about 10 minutes. Contact: 02 31 51 62 00, [Normandy American Cemetery and Memorial](www.abmc.gov).

Arromanches:

Visit Arromanches, the site of the ingenious Mulberry B artificial harbor—a testament to World War II engineering prowess. Observe the remains of the harbor in the water and on the beach. Experience the Arromanches 360 Circular Cinema, screening a 19-minute film with archival footage of the D-Day landings and the Battle of Normandy. Open daily from 9:30 am to 6 pm (or 7 pm from April to September), admission is €6.50 for adults, €5.50 for children, and

€6 for students and seniors. The cinema is located on the hill above Arromanches, accessible by car from the American Cemetery in about 25 minutes. Contact: 02 31 22 30 30, [Arromanches 360 Circular Cinema](www.arromanches360.com).

Gold Beach:

Explore Gold Beach, one of the two British sectors where the 50th Northumbrian Division landed. Witness the remains of the damaged Mulberry A harbor and the intact German coastal battery at Longues-sur-Mer. Visit the Gold Beach Museum, showcasing models, maps, photos, and objects related to the landing. Open daily from 10 am to 6 pm (or 7 pm from April to September), admission is €8 for adults, €5 for children, and €7 for students and seniors. The museum is located at Ver-sur-Mer, accessible by car from Arromanches in about 15 minutes. Contact: 02 31 22 58 58, [Gold Beach Museum](www.goldbeachmuseum.com).

Juno Beach:

Proceed to Juno Beach, the Canadian sector where the 3rd Canadian Infantry Division landed and encountered strong German opposition. Observe the remains of the Atlantic Wall fortifications, bunkers, and anti-tank obstacles. Visit the Juno Beach Centre, the only museum dedicated to the Canadian contribution to World War II. Open daily from 9:30 am to 6 pm (or 7 pm from April to September), admission is €9.50 for adults, €7.50 for children, and €8.50 for students and seniors. The center is located at Courseulles-sur-Mer, accessible by car from Gold Beach in about 20 minutes. Contact: 02 31 37 32 17, [Juno Beach Centre](www.junobeach.org).

Sword Beach:

Conclude your day at Sword Beach, the other British sector where the 3rd British Infantry Division landed. Witness the iconic Pegasus Bridge, the first objective of the British airborne forces on D-Day. Visit the Pegasus Memorial Museum, showcasing a replica of the original bridge, a glider, and various artifacts and documents related to the operation. Open daily from 10 am to 6 pm (or 6:30 pm from April to September), admission is €8 for adults, €5 for children, and €7 for students and seniors. The museum is near the bridge, accessible by car from Juno Beach in about 30 minutes. Contact: 02 31 78 19 44, [Pegasus Memorial Museum](www.musee-pegasus.com).

This concludes your second day in Normandy, where you've explored iconic D-Day sites and gained insights into the bravery and sacrifices of Allied troops. Revel in the scenic views and the charm of Normandy's coastal towns. Rest for the night in Bayeux, preparing for the adventures on your third day.

7.3 Day 3: Mont Saint-Michel

Embark on the third day of your Normandy adventure to witness one of France's most iconic treasures: Mont Saint-Michel. This medieval island abbey, a UNESCO World Heritage Site, is a testament to architectural brilliance, rich history, and profound spirituality. Explore the island and its captivating surroundings while marveling at the breathtaking tidal phenomena.

How to Get There:

If you're based in Bayeux, a scenic drive of about an hour and a half will take you to Mont Saint-Michel. Park your car at the mainland parking lot for 14.50 euros per day. From there, enjoy a picturesque 45-minute walk across the causeway or opt for the free shuttle bus, a convenient 15-minute ride. At the parking lot, you may also hire an electric car or a bicycle. For a hassle-free experience, consider joining a guided tour from Bayeux, including transportation, admission, and a knowledgeable guide.

What to See and Do:

The crowning jewel of Mont Saint-Michel is its abbey, a stunning fusion of Romanesque and Gothic architecture. Explore the abbey's history, symbolism, and hidden secrets at your own pace or with a guide. The abbey welcomes visitors daily from 9:30 am to 6 pm (May to August) and 9:30 am to 5 pm (September to April). Admission is 10 euros for adults, 8 euros for students, and free for children under 18. Get your tickets online ahead of time to avoid the lineup. Guided tours of the abbey, costing an additional 3 euros and lasting around an hour, offer deeper insights.

Beyond the abbey, discover other captivating attractions on Mont Saint-Michel, including the Maritime and Ecology Museum, the History Museum, Tiphaine's House, and the Archeoscope. These small museums provide insights into Mont Saint-Michel's life and history, such as tides, legends, wars, and art. Admission to each museum is 9 euros for adults, 5 euros for children, and free for those under 7. Opt for a combined ticket for all four museums at 18 euros for adults, 9 euros for children, and free for those under 7.

Stroll around the village and ramparts, immersing yourself in the views, atmosphere, and local shops. Purchase souvenirs like postcards, magnets, books, or regional products such as biscuits, cider, or cheese. Indulge in a culinary experience at one of the restaurants, savoring the renowned omelet of La Mère Poulard or the traditional lamb of the salt marshes.

Experience the natural wonder of the Mont Saint-Michel Bay, designated as a biosphere reserve. Witness the extraordinary tides, among the highest globally, transforming the landscape and access to the island. Explore the bay safely and enjoyably by joining a guided walk and learning about its ecology and history.

Where to Stay:

For a truly enchanting experience, consider staying overnight on the island. Revel in the tranquility and charm of Mont Saint-Michel after the day visitors have departed. Choose from hotels and guesthouses like Auberge Saint-Pierre, Hôtel la Croix Blanche, or La Mère Poulard. Prices range from 100 euros to 300 euros per night, depending on the season and accommodation type.

Alternatively, stay on the mainland and relish views of Mont Saint-Michel from a distance. Select from hotels and campsites near the parking lot, such as Hôtel Mercure Mont Saint-Michel, Hôtel Vert, or Camping Haliotis. Prices vary from 50 euros to 150 euros per night, contingent on the season and accommodation type.

Mont Saint-Michel promises to captivate you with its beauty, history, and spiritual essence—a place etched in your memory, beckoning you to return.

7.4 Day 4: Rouen

Embark on a journey through Rouen, the captivating capital of Normandy, renowned for its rich history, cultural treasures, and medieval charm. This city, often dubbed the "city of a hundred spires," stands as a testament to its numerous churches and cathedrals, earning it the title of the "city of art and history." Here's your guide to a fulfilling day in Rouen:

1. Cathédrale Notre-Dame de Rouen: Commence your day by exploring the awe-inspiring Cathédrale Notre-Dame de Rouen, a Gothic masterpiece dominating the skyline. With over a millennium of worship, art, and history, this historic church boasts three distinct towers, each showcasing a unique style. The cathedral's façade, immortalized by Claude Monet in his famous series, invites you to admire its changing light and colors. Explore the interior with its soaring nave, decorated choir, splendid organ, and a wealth of stained glass windows, sculptures, and paintings. Don't miss the Chapelle de la Vierge, housing a beautiful marble statue of the Virgin Mary. The cathedral is open daily, except Sundays and holidays, with free admission. Guided tours are available for a more in-depth experience.

2. Rue du Gros-Horloge: After marveling at the cathedral, stroll along the charming Rue du Gros-Horloge, a pedestrian street adorned with half-timbered houses, shops, cafés, and restaurants. Named after the 14th-century astronomical clock, one of Europe's oldest and most intricate, the street leads you to the belfry tower. Climb to the top for a panoramic view of the city and the cathedral. The clock and tower are open from Tuesday to Sunday.

3. Place du Vieux-Marché: Continue your walk to the heart of Rouen, the Place du Vieux-Marché. This historic square witnessed the tragic end of Joan of Arc in 1431. Visit the modern Église Sainte-Jeanne-d'Arc, built in her honor, featuring a distinctive design with an inverted boat-like roof. Explore the adjacent Historial Jeanne d'Arc, a multimedia museum retracing Joan of Arc's life and trial through projections, holograms, and sound effects.

4. Lunch at the Old Market Square: Choose from the restaurants and cafes surrounding the Place du Vieux-Marché for lunch. Delight in the local specialty, duckling à la rouennaise, a dish showcasing roasted duck with a distinctive blood and liver sauce. La Couronne, founded in 1345 and the oldest inn in France, is an excellent choice for a traditional and refined Norman cuisine experience.

5. Musée des Beaux-Arts de Rouen: Post-lunch, immerse yourself in art at the Musée des Beaux-Arts de Rouen, housed in a majestic building partially designed by Napoleon III. This museum boasts an extensive collection from the 15th to the 21st centuries, featuring works by renowned artists like Caravaggio, Rubens, Monet, and Picasso. A dedicated section highlights impressionist masterpieces, including Monet's famous paintings of Rouen Cathedral.

6. Additional Attractions: If time permits, explore other intriguing attractions in Rouen, such as the Musée de la Céramique, Musée Le Secq des Tournelles, Musée Flaubert et d'Histoire de la Médecine, or Musée National de l'Éducation.

7. Dinner at Rouen's Finest Restaurants: Conclude your day with a delightful dinner at one of Rouen's top restaurants. L'Odas, Origine, or the two-Michelin-starred Gill offer creative, refined, and locally inspired cuisines. Immerse yourself in the city's gastronomic excellence with an average meal price ranging from 50 to 100 euros per person.

Rouen beckons you with its blend of beauty, culture, and history, promising an enriching experience that resonates with the spirit and soul of Normandy.

7.5 Day 5: Honfleur and Deauville

Embark on the fifth day of your Normandy adventure, exploring the enchanting coastal towns of Honfleur and Deauville. These gems blend artistic heritage, maritime history, lively atmospheres, and glamorous styles.
Honfleur:

Commence your day in Honfleur, a quaint port town on the Seine estuary's southern bank. Admire the iconic half-timbered houses in vibrant hues lining the quays. Immerse yourself in the lively waterfront ambiance, indulging in local delicacies like seafood, cider, and calvados. A must-visit is the Sainte-Catherine Church, a unique wooden marvel resembling an inverted boat showcasing intricate paintings, sculptures, and stained glass. Explore Honfleur's art museums, including Musée Eugène Boudin, featuring works by Boudin, Monet, Courbet, and Jongkind. Nature enthusiasts can enjoy the stunning views by walking to the beach or visiting the Chapel of Notre Dame de Grâce. Don't miss a boat trip from Honfleur to witness the majestic Pont de Normandie.

Deauville:

In the afternoon, venture to Deauville, a chic seaside resort renowned for its sandy beach, elegant villas, casino, and international film festival. Stroll along the boardwalk adorned with colorful parasols and wooden cabins, where the names of visiting stars are immortalized. Indulge in beach activities, from swimming to horse riding. Deauville's boutiques, art galleries, and markets offer diverse shopping experiences. Explore the glamour of Casino Barrière, featuring various games and entertainment. Culminate your day with a gastronomic journey, savoring Normandy's sophistication and diversity in restaurants like Le Spinnaker, La Flambée, and Le Ciro's.

We trust this guide provides you with a delightful itinerary for discovering Honfleur and Deauville's charm, culture, and beauty. May your day in these picturesque towns be truly unforgettable!

7.6 Day 6: Bayeux

On your sixth day in Normandy, dive into the allure of Bayeux, a captivating town serving as an ideal hub for exploring the historic D-Day beaches and the iconic Mont-Saint-Michel. Bayeux, rich in history and culture, boasts a magnificent cathedral, a world-renowned tapestry, and a vibrant market. Additionally, you have the opportunity to pay homage to the Bayeux War Cemetery, the largest British cemetery in France from World War II. Here's a detailed guide on maximizing your day in Bayeux:

Commence your day with a visit to the Bayeux Cathedral, an exquisite example of Gothic architecture dating back to the 11th century. This cathedral, once home to the renowned Bayeux Tapestry, witnessed the coronation of William the Conqueror as King of England in 1066. Immerse yourself in the grandeur of the impressive façade, stained glass windows, crypt, and treasury. The cathedral offers free admission daily from 8:30 am to 6 pm. To make the most of your visit, consider renting an audio guide for 3 euros per person or participating in a guided tour, which cost 5 euros each. You can make reservations for these options on their website or by phoning +33 2 31 92 01 33.

Continue your exploration by heading to the Bayeux Tapestry Museum, home to the iconic Bayeux Tapestry – an embroidered fabric spanning 70 meters that tells the story of the events leading up to the Norman invasion of England in 1066. A 16-language audio tour narrates the story of the tapestry, which is recognized as a UNESCO World Heritage Site. The museum, open daily from 9 am to 6:30 pm, charges an admission fee of 10 euros per adult and 5 euros per child, with free entry for children under 10. Secure your tickets on their website or by calling +33 2 31 51 25 50.

Following lunch, pay your respects at the Bayeux War Cemetery, the largest British cemetery in France from World War II. Housing the graves of 4,648 soldiers predominantly from the United Kingdom, it stands as a solemn tribute to the sacrifices made during the Normandy liberation. The cemetery, open from dawn to dusk daily, offers free admission. Take a moment to visit the nearby Bayeux Memorial, honoring 1,808 Commonwealth soldiers with no known grave. Additional information is available on their website.

Conclude your day with a stroll through the Bayeux Market, a highlight among Normandy's best markets. Held every Saturday morning on Place Saint-Patrice and surrounding streets, this market showcases various products, including cheese, cider, seafood, meat, fruits, and pastries. Engage with friendly vendors eager to share their stories and recipes. The market operates from 8 am to 1 pm, conveniently located near the city center and its attractions.

These experiences represent a glimpse into Bayeux's blend of history, culture, and gastronomy. For more options and reviews, refer to platforms like Tripadvisor. Regardless of your choices, Bayeux promises a day of enjoyment in one of Normandy's most captivating towns.

7.7 Day 7: Departure

As your 7-day journey in Normandy, a region that enchanted you with its historical richness, cultural tapestry, and natural splendor, concludes, it's time to bid farewell and return home. Throughout your exploration, you've immersed yourself in iconic sites like the D-Day Landing Beaches, the Bay of Mont-Saint-Michel, the Alabaster Coast, and the hidden gems like Monet's Garden, Château de Falaise, Camembert Village, and La Colline aux Oiseaux. Your taste buds have savored the delightful flavors of Normandy – from cider and cheese to apple tart and seafood. The warm and friendly atmosphere, coupled with the hospitality of the locals, has made your time in Normandy truly memorable, imparting values of Reconciliation, Peace, and Freedom.

As you plan your journey back home, here are some convenient options based on your departure airport:
Paris Charles de Gaulle Airport (CDG):

- Take a train from Caen to Paris Saint-Lazare station (2 hours, approx. 30 euros per person).
- Transfer to RER B line from Saint-Lazare to Charles de Gaulle Airport (50 minutes, approx. 10 euros per person).

- Alternatively, opt for a direct bus from Caen to Charles de Gaulle Airport (4 hours, approx. 20 euros per person).

Paris Orly Airport (ORY):

- Take a train from Caen to Paris Saint-Lazare station (2 hours, approx. 30 euros per person).
- Switch to RER C line from Saint-Lazare to Pont de Rungis-Aéroport d'Orly station (40 minutes, approx. 6 euros per person).
- Take a shuttle bus from Pont de Rungis-Aéroport d'Orly station to Orly Airport (15 minutes, approx. 2 euros per person).
- Alternatively, consider a direct bus from Caen to Orly Airport (4 hours, approx. 20 euros per person).

Beauvais-Tillé Airport:

- Take a train from Caen to Beauvais station (3 hours, approx. 40 euros per person).
- Transfer to a shuttle bus from Beauvais station to Beauvais-Tillé Airport (15 minutes, approx. 4 euros per person).
- You can explore Normandy Tourism or France-Voyage websites for more transportation options, including car rentals, taxis, or private transfers.

Additionally, local tourist offices can provide valuable information and assistance.

As your 7-day adventure in Normandy concludes, we trust this guide has not only aided in planning your trip but has also provided an enjoyable read. Thank you for choosing Normandy as your destination and for having Copilot as your companion. Wishing you a safe and pleasant journey back home, and we look forward to welcoming you again, whether in Normandy or another captivating destination. Au revoir et à bientôt!

Chapter 8: Practical Information and Tips

8.1 Transportation

Normandy, situated in northern France, is effortlessly accessible and navigable, thanks to its well-established transportation network. Whether you opt for planes, trains, buses, cars, or bikes, various transportation modes cater to diverse budgets and preferences, facilitating your exploration of this picturesque region. Consider these insights to streamline your transportation plans in Normandy:

By Plane: Normandy boasts two international airports: Caen-Carpiquet Airport and Deauville-Normandie Airport. These hubs connect to multiple destinations across France and Europe, including Paris, Lyon, London, Dublin, and Amsterdam. Paris-Charles de Gaulle Airport or Paris-Orly Airport also serve as major gateways, with convenient train or bus connections to Normandy.

By Train: A well-developed rail network interconnects Normandy's main cities like Rouen, Caen, Le Havre, Cherbourg, and Bayeux. High-speed trains (TGV) from Paris to Normandy take approximately 2 hours. Get train tickets at the station or online, and take advantage of early booking or rail pass discounts.

By Bus: Normandy features several bus companies offering affordable and comfortable travel between cities and regions, including Flixbus services from Paris. One-way tickets range between 10 and 20 euros, taking 3 to 5 hours. Discounts are available for early bookings or with a student card.

By Car: Navigate Normandy's scenic landscapes and attractions through its well-maintained road network. Car rental agencies abound, allowing you to explore at your own pace. Ensure a valid driver's license, insurance, and registration document. Some highways may require tolls, and adherence to speed limits and traffic rules is essential.

By Bike: For a unique exploration experience, Normandy offers diverse cycling routes suitable for various levels and interests. Coastal paths, countryside trails, and city circuits allow you to discover the region's beauty and history. Rent a bike from local shops or bring your own if traveling by train or bus. Helmets, locks, and repair kits are essential, and adhering to cycling paths and respecting pedestrians and drivers is crucial.

Transportation shapes your Normandy experience, influencing your time, budget, and enjoyment. Select the form of transportation that best suits your needs and ensures a smooth and pleasurable discovery of Normandy's attractions. It's not just a means of getting around; it's a way to uncover the essence of Normandy, making your trip more accessible and enjoyable.

8.2 Health and Safety

Normandy stands out as a secure and inviting region in France, promising a vacation filled with relaxation and fulfillment. Nonetheless, being mindful of potential health and safety concerns is crucial, like any journey. Here are some practical tips to ensure a healthy and safe experience during your visit to Normandy:

Healthcare: Benefit from France's high-quality healthcare system, covering public and private facilities. European Union citizens can access services with the European Health Insurance Card (EHIC). Non-EU citizens may need to pay upfront, seeking reimbursement from travel insurance or their home country. A comprehensive travel insurance policy is recommended, covering medical expenses and other risks.

Pharmacies: Identify pharmacies by green cross sign, typically open from 9 am to 7 pm, Monday to Saturday. Some may offer 24-hour service or Sunday openings. Pharmacies provide prescription and over-the-counter medications, along with health and beauty products. A prescription might be necessary for certain medicines, and pharmacists can advise on minor ailments.

Emergencies:

Know the emergency contact numbers:
- 112: European emergency number for all emergencies.
- 15: Medical emergency service (SAMU) for an ambulance or medical assistance.
- 17: Police for crimes, violence, or public order issues.
- 18: Fire brigade, handling emergencies like floods, gas leaks, or animal rescue.

Crime: While Normandy is generally safe, be cautious against common crimes like pickpocketing. Be vigilant in crowded places, avoid displaying valuable items, and stay cautious of unsolicited offers. Report any crimes to the nearest police station, obtaining a copy for insurance or embassy purposes.

Road Safety:

Explore Normandy's well-connected road network with these safety tips:
- Drive on the right, overtake on the left.
- Wear seat belts and helmets as required.
- Adhere to speed limits, adjusting for weather and road conditions.
- Avoid mobile phone use while driving.
- Never drive under the influence of alcohol or drugs.

- Possess valid documents, including a driver's license, insurance, and registration.
- Carry mandatory vehicle equipment and be familiar with road signs.

These guidelines ensure a healthy and safe journey through Normandy. With its welcoming locals, accessible healthcare, and secure environment, Normandy provides a home-like atmosphere for travelers. Preparedness and vigilance will enable you to revel in your Normandy adventure worry-free, creating cherished and memorable moments.

8.3 Local Customs and Etiquette

Normandy, boasting a diverse culture shaped by its maritime setting, agricultural heritage, and historical connections, invites travelers to embrace local customs and etiquette for a more enriching experience. Here are essential tips for a pleasant stay in Normandy and respectful interactions with the locals:

Greetings:

Commence interactions with a friendly "Bonjour" or "Bonsoir," complemented by a handshake or two to three cheek kisses, depending on the region. "Salut" is suitable for friends or young individuals, but exercise caution with strangers or older acquaintances. Farewells can be expressed with "Au revoir" or "À bientôt."

Titles:

When addressing individuals, use titles and last names like "Monsieur Dupont" or "Madame Martin." "Mademoiselle" is appropriate for young unmarried women, but refrain from using it for older or married women. Employ "tu" for friends or close relatives and "vous" for strangers, older individuals, or superiors, switching to "tu" if invited or in close relationships.

Dining:

Normandy's renowned cuisine is best enjoyed with proper etiquette:

- Wait for the host or eldest person to say "Bon appétit" before starting.
- Keep hands visible on the table, using the napkin appropriately.
- Follow cutlery usage, express appreciation for the food, and avoid leaving anything uneaten.
- Toasting is customary; wait for someone to propose a toast, maintain eye contact, and say "Santé" or "À votre santé."
- Tipping is unnecessary in restaurants as service is included; rounding up the bill is appreciated.

Dress:

Normandy's climate, characterized by mild seasons, warrants layered dressing and the inclusion of rain gear. Opt for modest and casual attire, avoiding flashy or revealing clothing. Jeans, sweaters, and jackets are suitable, but steer clear of shorts, tank tops, or flip-flops. When entering a church or public building, remove hats or scarves.

Gifts:

Normandy's hospitality is well-reflected in the tradition of bringing a gift when visiting:

- Choose thoughtful, simple gifts like wine, chocolates, or flowers.
- Consider bringing something representative of your country or region.
- Avoid extravagant gifts, opting for gestures that express gratitude.
- Sending a thank-you note post-visit is a courteous practice.

This guide aims to help you navigate Normandy's social norms, ensuring a culturally sensitive experience. The locals, known for their friendliness, will appreciate your efforts to embrace their traditions and customs. Enjoy your time in Normandy!

Conclusion

As you conclude this Normandy Travel Guide, we trust that the journey through its pages has been as delightful for you as it has been for us to compose. With its breathtaking landscapes, rich history, vibrant culture, and delectable cuisine, Normandy offers a myriad of experiences. Whether you seek a tranquil retreat, thrilling exploration, or a meaningful commemoration, Normandy caters to every traveler.

Throughout this guide, we aim to furnish you with the most pertinent and up-to-date information for your 2024 Normandy excursion. We covered optimal visitation times, guidance on transportation, and detailed insights into Normandy's key regions. A suggested 7-day itinerary was outlined, encompassing the region's highlights, complemented by valuable travel tips and recommendations.

However, this guide is merely a starting point, and Normandy holds even more treasures to uncover. For additional options and reviews, platforms like Tripadvisor or other travel websites can offer valuable insights. Watch for events in 2024, such as the 80th anniversary of D-Day and the Battle of Normandy, the Deauville American Film Festival, and the Tall Ships' Races.

We aspire that this guide sparks the desire to explore Normandy, a region renowned in France for its beauty and diversity. We are confident that your time in Normandy will be nothing short of splendid, and we eagerly anticipate hearing about your experiences. Feel free to share your feedback, photos, and stories with us on our website or social media. Thank you for choosing Normandy Travel Guide, and may your journey be filled with bon voyage!

Printed in Great Britain
by Amazon

41260362R00069